CHAPTER 1

KINDS OF GOVERNMENT

English thinker **John Locke** said we have a right to protect the rights we are born with. The **American Revolution** acted on that idea! The Founding Fathers said people as a group can choose whatever government they think will best protect those rights. But what are the choices? What are the ways people have organized themselves to make their own rules and protections? Chester and his friends get a chance to try different governments on a distant planet with an unfriendly alien . . .

next: REPUBLICS CAN

CHESTER THE CRAB
WHAT IS REPRESENTATIVE DEMOCRACY?

CHESTER IS HELPING 23 THIRD-GRADERS FORM A GOVERNMENT ON A DISTANT PLANET.

YES HE IS! YOU KNOW IT.

I'M NOT SURE, BECAUSE YOU DON'T KNOW THAT!!

WE'LL NEVER GET OFF THIS MUDBALL!

TALK TO THE HAND, BABY!

ARE YOU KIDDING? NO WAY IS HE...

YOU HAVE NO IDEA HOW...

IF WE DON'T WE'LL NEVER...

THERE IS ONLY ONE WAY OUT!

I WON'T GO WITH THAT PLAN.

WHY NOT??!!

QUIET!

I CAN'T HEAR MYSELF THINK!!

BOYD '02

THIS IS A COMMON PROBLEM IN SOCIALISM AND IN DEMOCRACY (A GOVERNMENT WHERE EVERY CITIZEN VOTES ON **ALL** DECISIONS).

BUT GIVING EVERYONE AN EQUAL VOTE SEEMS FAIR.

YES, BUT GOVERNMENT MUST ALSO GET THINGS DONE. AT THIS RATE, WE'LL DIE OF THIRST BEFORE WE AGREE ON A PLAN.

LET'S TRY ORGANIZING OURSELVES AS A **REPUBLIC**. IT USES DEMOCRACY ON TWO LEVELS.

FIRST, EVERYONE VOTES FOR FIVE REPRESENTATIVES OUT OF THIS CLASS OF 23 KIDS AND ONE CRAB.

THE SECOND LEVEL OF **REPRESENTATIVE DEMOCRACY** IS: THE FIVE MAKE RULES AND DECISIONS FOR ALL 24. WE AGREE TO DO WHAT THEY DECIDE.

ALL IN FAVOR OF LOOKING FOR WATER THAT WAY?

AYE!
AYE!
AYE!
AYE!

MAJORITY RULES IN THE 4-1 VOTE, SO THE CLASS SEARCHES:

HEY HAS ANYONE NOTICED THAT WE ARE STANDING ON...

...EARTH AGAIN, THANKS TO THAT WEIRD ALIEN TRANSPORT DEVICE?!

YAAAY!

END

THE LAWMAKERS

The government of the United States has **three branches: the legislative** to make the laws, **the executive** to enforce the laws, and **the judicial** to review how those laws are working. The way the legislative branch works an idea into a law can be long and confusing. Our government has a lot of **checks and balances** to keep bad ideas from becoming laws . . .

WHO MAKES THE RULES?

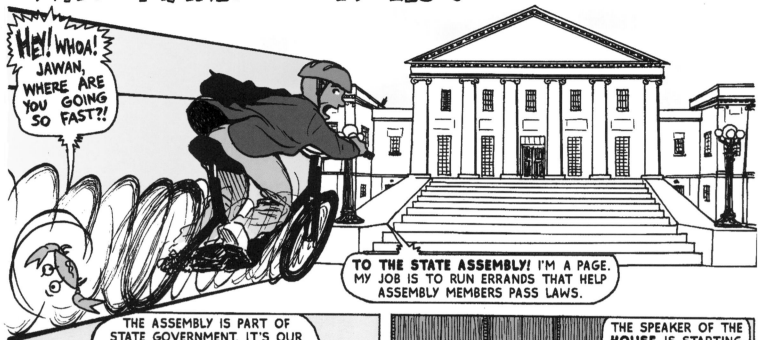

HEY! WHOA! JAWAN, WHERE ARE YOU GOING SO FAST?!

TO THE STATE ASSEMBLY! I'M A PAGE. MY JOB IS TO RUN ERRANDS THAT HELP ASSEMBLY MEMBERS PASS LAWS.

THE ASSEMBLY IS PART OF STATE GOVERNMENT. IT'S OUR **LEGISLATURE**. IT PASSES LAWS THAT APPLY TO THE WHOLE STATE.

YOU MUST BE VERY HONORED!

RIGHT NOW I'M VERY **LATE**!

THE SPEAKER OF THE **HOUSE** IS STARTING TODAY'S BUSINESS IN THIS HALF OF THE ASSEMBLY!

(THE OTHER HALF OF THE ASSEMBLY IS THE **SENATE**.)

MR. SPEAKER, AT THE REQUEST OF THE PEOPLE WHO ELECTED ME, I SUBMIT A BILL TO REQUIRE THAT BICYCLES HAVE SOLAR POWER.

DELEGATE RAY'S BILL IS ORDERED PRINTED AND SENT TO THE HOUSE COMMITTEE ON TRANSPORTATION.

AND WHO WILL TRANSPORT IT? ME!

next: COMMITTED

BOYD '00

WHAT GETS COMMITTED IN COMMITTEE?

OOF HERE ARE... COPIES OF THE BILL REQUIRING BIKES...*whew:* TO HAVE SOLAR POWER.

A TALKING BLUE CRAB?!!

ACTUALLY, JAWAN SAID THAT.

I THOUGHT THE WHOLE ASSEMBLY DEBATED EACH BILL. BUT MOST OF THE DEBATE IS DONE IN ITS **COMMITTEES** — GROUPS OF A FEW LEGISLATORS STUDYING ONE TOPIC.

TRANSPORTATION COMMITTEE

IT'S A BIG JOB DECIDING WHICH BILLS SHOULD BECOME LAWS. **LAWS** ARE MADE TO HELP PEOPLE KNOW WHAT THEY SHOULD AND SHOULD NOT DO. AND PEOPLE OFTEN DISAGREE ON THE "SHOULDS."

DELEGATES, BIKES COULD USE SOLAR POWER TO GET UP BIG HILLS WHEN A RIDER'S LEGS ARE TIRED.

BUT THE EXTRA SOLAR EQUIPMENT WILL MAKE BIKES HEAVIER AND HARDER TO PEDAL!

hmmm, MAYBE WE SHOULD TABLE THIS BILL SO IT DIES IN COMMITTEE...

MR. CHAIRMAN, I CALL FOR A VOTE.

YES, LET'S VOTE.

ALL THOSE IN FAVOR SAY:

AYE!

next: CHANGE IS GONNA COME

WHO CAN AMEND WHAT THEY MEANT?

SOMEWHERE IN THE STATE'S ASSEMBLY...

... AND WHEREAS BICYCLISTS WHO CAN'T GET UP BIG HILLS GET ALL WOBBLY AND ARE A DANGER TO JOGGERS, CARS, AND SQUIRRELS, BE IT RESOLVED THAT ALL BIKES SOLD IN THIS STATE SHOULD HAVE SOLAR POWER AS BACKUP.

THAT WAS THE SECOND READING OF THE BILL TO THE ASSEMBLY'S HOUSE. NOW IT IS OPEN SEASON!

OPEN SEASON?

I WILL ENTERTAIN ANY QUESTIONS THE HOUSE MAY HAVE ABOUT MY BILL.

AMENDMENT

AMENDMENT

AMENDMENT

yikes

OTHER REPRESENTATIVES ARE TRYING TO CHANGE — OR AMEND — MR. RAY'S BILL. MY JOB IS TO COPY AMENDMENTS SO THE PEOPLE CAN DEBATE THEM.

LET'S COPY MY CLAWS NEXT!

AYE

Nay

Nay

THE AMENDMENT TO TAKE OUT THE WORDS "SOLD IN RETAIL STORES" IS APPROVED.

THE AMENDMENT TO ADD "AND MOTORCYCLES" IS DEFEATED.

THE AMENDMENT TO ADD "HURT KITTY-WITTYS" IS DEFEATED.

I CALL FOR THE VOTE! PLEASE!! BEFORE SOMEONE ELSE TWISTS MY BILL ANOTHER WAY!!

BILL 8755 IS APPROVED ON THIRD READING, 57 TO 43.

SO NOW IT'S A LAW!

NOT YET!

next: SENT TO SENATE

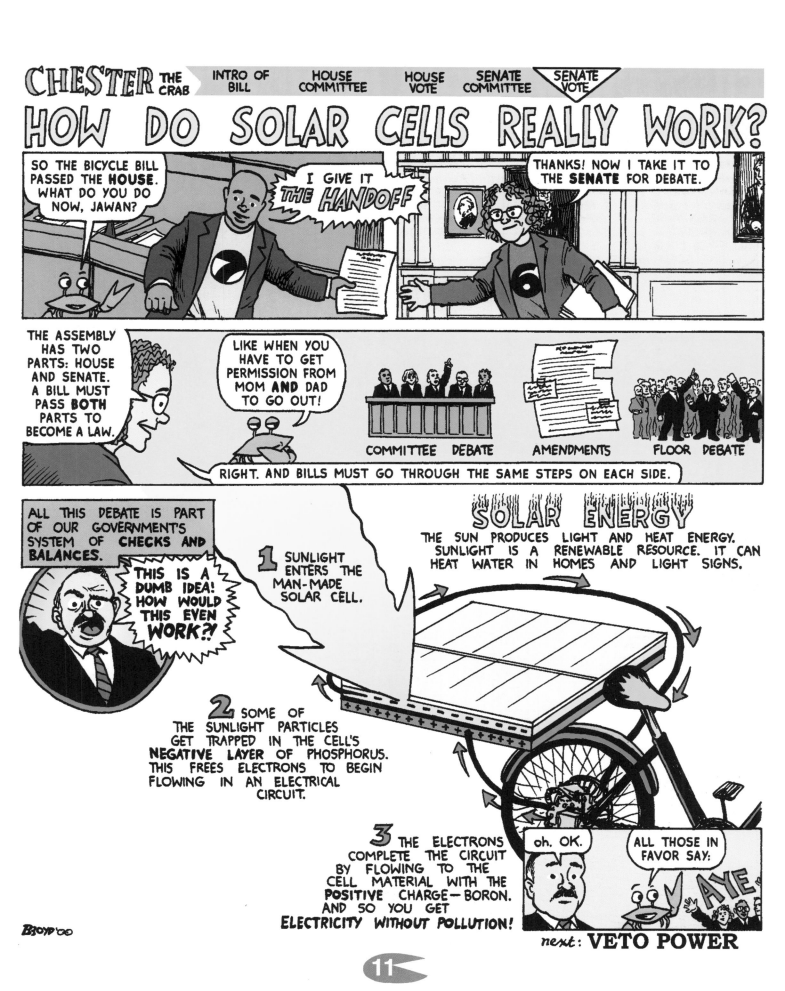

HOW DO SOLAR CELLS REALLY WORK?

SO THE BICYCLE BILL PASSED THE **HOUSE**. WHAT DO YOU DO NOW, JAWAN?

I GIVE IT *THE HANDOFF*

THANKS! NOW I TAKE IT TO THE **SENATE** FOR DEBATE.

THE ASSEMBLY HAS TWO PARTS: HOUSE AND SENATE. A BILL MUST PASS **BOTH** PARTS TO BECOME A LAW.

LIKE WHEN YOU HAVE TO GET PERMISSION FROM MOM **AND** DAD TO GO OUT!

COMMITTEE DEBATE

AMENDMENTS

FLOOR DEBATE

RIGHT. AND BILLS MUST GO THROUGH THE SAME STEPS ON EACH SIDE.

ALL THIS DEBATE IS PART OF OUR GOVERNMENT'S SYSTEM OF **CHECKS AND BALANCES**.

THIS IS A DUMB IDEA! HOW WOULD THIS EVEN **WORK?!**

SOLAR ENERGY

THE SUN PRODUCES LIGHT AND HEAT ENERGY. SUNLIGHT IS A RENEWABLE RESOURCE. IT CAN HEAT WATER IN HOMES AND LIGHT SIGNS.

1 SUNLIGHT ENTERS THE MAN-MADE SOLAR CELL.

2 SOME OF THE SUNLIGHT PARTICLES GET TRAPPED IN THE CELL'S **NEGATIVE** LAYER OF PHOSPHORUS. THIS FREES ELECTRONS TO BEGIN FLOWING IN AN ELECTRICAL CIRCUIT.

3 THE ELECTRONS COMPLETE THE CIRCUIT BY FLOWING TO THE CELL MATERIAL WITH THE **POSITIVE** CHARGE—BORON. AND SO YOU GET **ELECTRICITY WITHOUT POLLUTION!**

oh. OK.

ALL THOSE IN FAVOR SAY: AYE

next: **VETO POWER**

BBOYD '00

11

PRESIDENTIAL ELECTION

One of the most important things a United States citizen can do to help run the government is to **vote in elections** at the local, state, and national level. The election that everyone can vote on is the race for **president**. Every four years men and women compete to see who will lead our **executive branch**. But this is no simple popularity contest. The Founding Fathers put in an important twist: the **electoral college** . . .

WHO REPRESENTS IN AMERICA?

OK, **FINE!** I'LL JUST GO WHERE **I** WANT TO GO!!

WHAZZZUP TAMARA?

GRrrRR!! NONE OF MY FRIENDS CAN AGREE WHERE WE SHOULD RIDE.

MAYBE YOU HAD TOO MANY DEBATING THE DESTINATION.

MAYBE. WE JUST WEREN'T GETTING ANYWHERE. AND I WANT TO **RIDE!**

THAT'S THE TROUBLE WITH **DIRECT DEMOCRACY.** IT CAN GET MESSY.

DEMOCRACY? LIKE WHEN WE WENT TO **ANCIENT GREECE?**

RIGHT! GREEK MEN WHO WERE CITIZENS MET IN A FIELD TO DECIDE **LAWS** (RULES) FOR THEIR CITY. EACH MAN GOT ONE VOTE. IDEAS GETTING THE MOST VOTES BECAME LAWS.

IN COLONIAL AMERICA, NEW ENGLANDERS USED DIRECT DEMOCRACY IN **TOWN MEETINGS.** BUT THIS WOULDN'T WORK ACROSS THE WHOLE UNITED STATES.

CAN YOU HEAR ME IN THE BACK?

SO THE **U.S. CONSTITUTION** OF 1787 USES **REPRESENTATIVE DEMOCRACY.** EACH AMERICAN CITIZEN STILL GETS ONE VOTE — TO ELECT SOMEONE WHO WILL DEBATE THE LAWS **FOR** HIM OR HER.

TODAY A REPRESENTATIVE IN CONGRESS SPEAKS FOR HUNDREDS OF THOUSANDS OF PEOPLE.

U.S. CAPITOL

DRIVE THRU

MY VOTERS WANT FRIES WITH THAT LAW.

next: X

CHESTER THE CRAB
WHO THROWS POLITICAL PARTIES?

CHESTER IS RIDING WITH THIRD GRADER TAMARA...

I KEEP HEARING ABOUT A PRESIDENTIAL RACE. IS THAT GOING TO BE ON ESPN?

BOYD '00

THE PRESIDENTIAL RACE IS JUST AHEAD! WE CAN CATCH IT!

THE **PRESIDENT** IS THE TOP **EXECUTIVE** IN THE FEDERAL GOVERNMENT. HE REPRESENTS EVERY UNITED STATES CITIZEN.

AAAAAH!! THIRD PARTY CANDIDATE!!!

uhh... SO WHICH OF THESE GUYS IS PRESIDENT?

EVERY FOUR YEARS THESE GUYS (AND OTHERS) RACE TO BE PRESIDENT. THESE TWO CHARACTERS **SYMBOLIZE** THE TWO BIGGEST POLITICAL GROUPS IN THE U.S.

SINCE 1837 THE DONKEY HAS STOOD FOR **DEMOCRATS**. THESE CANDIDATES TEND TO BE LIBERAL, PUSHING GOVERNMENT TO HELP PEOPLE.

SINCE 1874 THE ELEPHANT HAS STOOD FOR **REPUBLICANS**. THESE CANDIDATES TEND TO BE CONSERVATIVE, FAVORING BUSINESS OVER GOVERNMENT.

AND A THIRD PARTY MESSES UP **OUR** POWER. WHAT PARTY IS A **CRAB**, ANYWAY?!

IT'S ... um.. "THE **ENVIRONMENTALS**!"

ALSO KNOWN AS "THE GARDEN PARTY"!

POLITICAL PARTIES ORGANIZE VOTERS WHO BELIEVE THE SAME THINGS. PARTIES BRING TOGETHER CANDIDATES, MONEY, AND VOTERS. THAT'S HOW TO WIN.

HOW DO WE WIN, CHESTER ??

next: PRIMARY COLORS

HOW DO PARTIES PICK CANDIDATES?

PEOPLE IN THE UNITED STATES PICK A PRESIDENT EVERY FOUR YEARS. IT TAKES A LOT OF TIME AND MONEY, TAMARA.

1 THE RACE STARTS WHEN MEN AND WOMEN ANNOUNCE THEY WILL BE A **CANDIDATE**. A NATURAL-BORN U.S. CITIZEN WHO IS AT LEAST 35 YEARS OLD CAN RUN (or bike) FOR PRESIDENT. CANDIDATES THEN START ASKING FOR **MONEY**.

I·· I'VE RAISED ONLY A FEW THOUSAND BUCKS SINCE I ANNOUNCED. I CAN'T PAY FOR CAMPAIGN WORKERS. I'M OUT.

2 THE MAJOR POLITICAL PARTIES — THE **DEMOCRATS** AND THE **REPUBLICANS** — HAVE **PRIMARIES** OR **CAUCUSES** IN EACH STATE. THIS IS THE FIRST CHANCE VOTERS GET TO PICK A PRESIDENTIAL CANDIDATE.

NOT ENOUGH VOTERS PICKED ME. I'M OUT.

3 THE CANDIDATE WHO WINS THE MOST VOTES IN PRIMARIES AND CAUCUSES BECOMES THE OFFICIAL CANDIDATE OF HIS OR HER PARTY. THIS DEAL IS SEALED AT THE PARTY'S **CONVENTION**.

next: Race For the College

I RAN FOR PRESIDENT IN **1800** WITHOUT LEAVING MY HOUSE OR BEGGING FOR MONEY. NOW CANDIDATES SPEND $**70** MILLION OR **MORE** TO BE PRESIDENT!!

DEMOCRATS FOR SMITH

REPUBLICANS FOR JONES

WHO GOES TO ELECTORAL COLLEGE?

THIRD GRADER TAMARA AND CHESTER ARE IN A RACE WITH THE **REPUBLICAN** ELEPHANT AND **DEMOCRATIC** DONKEY...

IN MOST AMERICAN ELECTIONS, THE CANDIDATE WITH THE MOST VOTES WINS. THE ELECTION FOR **PRESIDENT** HAS A *TWIST!!*

YAA

THE U.S. CONSTITUTION SAYS **ELECTORS** FROM EACH STATE ELECT A PRESIDENT.

eleXtoral college

N.Y.   TEXAS

WHAT ABOUT VOTERS?!

ELECTORS **ARE** LINKED TO REAL VOTERS.

LET'S SAY MOST VOTERS IN OHIO PICK THE REPUBLICAN FOR PRESIDENT. **ALL** OF OHIO'S 20 ELECTORS GO TO THE REPUBLICAN IN THE "WINNER TAKE ALL" RULE. THESE ELECTORS THEN VOTE FOR PRESIDENT. IT'S JUST MORE **REPRESENTATIVE DEMOCRACY.**

VERMONT   IDAHO   N.C.   LOUISIANA

OHIO

SO IF I GET 48% OF ALL THE MOMS AND DADS VOTING IN OHIO, I **DON'T** GET 48% OF OHIO'S ELECTORS. I LOSE THE WHOLE STATE!!

*MAINE AND NEBRASKA ARE DIFFERENT. THEY NAME ELECTORS FOR CANDIDATES THAT WIN CONGRESSIONAL DISTRICTS.

THIS IS WHY THIRD POLITICAL PARTIES NEVER ELECT A PRESIDENT. THEY WIN **VOTES** BUT **NOT ELECTORS!**

THE BIGGER THE STATE POPULATION, THE MORE ELECTORS IT HAS. DEMOCRATS AND REPUBLICANS FIGHT OVER BIG STATES BECAUSE WINNING THOSE ELECTORS QUICKLY ADDS UP.

CALIFORNIA

I NEED 270 ELECTORS TO WIN THE PRESIDENCY!

THESE 55 ELECTORS ARE MINE!!

BOYD '00

WHAMMO

next: MUDSLINGING

PRESIDENTIAL CABINET

One of the most dramatic changes in the United States government over the past 200 years is the growth of the **executive branch**. The number of people who help the **president** enact the laws and run the day-to-day operations of the federal government has grown from a few thousand to millions because Americans expect more and more services from their government. Here is how a president organizes all his workers . . .

WHO IS IN THE PRESIDENT'S CABINET?

I CAN'T EVEN BELIEVE MY MOM IS MAKING ME GO FURNITURE SHOPPING.

I HOPE WE'RE GOING TO "CRAB AND BARREL!"

MORE LIKE THE TV SHOW "FLIPPIN' HOUSE." SHE'S ALL IN TO USING ANTIQUES TO REDO ROOMS, AND NOW SHE'S AFTER MINE.

LAME.

LAME.

LAME.

Presidential Cabinet

HEY, LOOK AT THIS PIECE! IT HAS LOTS OF LITTLE DRAWERS.

IS THERE MONEY INSIDE?

Yes!

YAAAH!!

I'M THE SECRETARY OF THE TREASURY FOR THE UNITED STATES. MY DEPARTMENT WAS ONE OF THE FIRST EVER CREATED FOR THE NATION'S EXECUTIVE BRANCH. I MAKE OUR MONEY!!

Department of the Treasury Est. 1789

WHA — YOU... CHESTER, I THINK SOMEONE LEFT THEIR ACTION FIGURE BEHIND.

FIRST TREASURY SECRETARY WAS ALEXANDER HAMILTON, WHO **WAS** A MAN OF ACTION: HIS DEPARTMENT COLLECTED **TAXES** FOR THE NEW FEDERAL GOVERNMENT.

WAIT, SO THIS WAS **GEORGE WASHINGTON'S** FURNITURE?

YES — AND EACH PRESIDENT SINCE!

Constitution

THE **CONSTITUTION** OF 1787 SAID THE EXECUTIVE BRANCH CARRIES OUT THE LEGISLATIVE BRANCH'S LAWS — BUT IT DIDN'T SAY MUCH ABOUT **HOW** IT WOULD. WASHINGTON STARTED WITH FOUR DEPARTMENTS AND FEWER THAN 1,000 EMPLOYEES — NOW THERE ARE 15 DEPARTMENTS WITH OVER **4 MILLION WORKERS!**

I STILL DON'T GET WHY YOU'RE IN A CABINET THOUGH ...

next: EduMACaTion

WHO PROMOTES THE GENERAL WELFARE?

SO THE PRESIDENT HAS A LOT OF ADVISORS. I STILL DON'T GET WHY THEY'RE CALLED HIS "CABINET."

I HAVE ANSWERS! KING CHARLES 1 TOOK OVER ENGLAND IN 1625 AND HAD WEEKLY PRIVATE MEETINGS WITH A SMALL GROUP OF EXPERTS HE NAMED HIS "CABINET" — A FRENCH WORD FOR A SMALL, PRIVATE ROOM.

JAMES MADISON BORROWS THAT ENGLISH TRADITION WHEN HE USES "CABINET" IN 1793 TO REFER TO PRESIDENT GEORGE WASHINGTON'S TOP OFFICIALS IN THE EXECUTIVE BRANCH.

Department of Education
Est. 1980

Department of Defense 1789

SO THEY WERE HIS CLOSEST ADVISORS.

OR HIS CLOSET ADVISORS!

LEGISLATIVE   JUDICIAL   EXECUTIVE

BALLOT

IN OUR GOVERNMENT'S CHECKS AND BALANCES, THE UNITED STATES SENATE CONFIRMS A PRESIDENT'S PICK FOR A CABINET JOB. MAJORITY APPROVAL OF THE SENATE IS NEEDED TO GET A CABINET JOB!

SO VOTING FOR A SENATOR IS A CRITICAL CHOICE!

SURE THERE'S A LOT AT STAKE! LOOK AT ME: I AIM TO GET A DECENT, SAFE, CLEAN HOME FOR EVERY AMERICAN.

WILL YOU CLEAN MY ROOM?

CEMENT

Department of Housing and Urban Development
Est. 1966

I HAVE 10,000 EMPLOYEES AND A YEARLY BUDGET OF $32 BILLION! I BUILD AFFORDABLE HOUSING, NOT PICK UP DIRTY SOCKS!!

HMMPF. I HAVE MORE ACCESSORIES THAN THAT. I GET 400,000 EMPLOYEES AND $62 BILLION TO KEEP FOOD SAFE AND TO RESEARCH NEW MEDICINES.

Department of Health and Human Services
Est. 1953

PART OF MY JOB IS TO RUN MEDICARE HEALTH SERVICES FOR THE ELDERLY AND MEDICAID FOR THE POOR.

CHESTER, WHY WOULD I BUY FURNITURE THAT IS ALREADY ... FULL?

THE FOLKS IN THE NEXT FEW DRAWERS WILL PROTECT WHATEVER ELSE YOU HAVE IN YOUR ROOM!

next: D-

WHO PLAYS DEFENSE FOR STATE?

CHESTER AND JAWAN HAVE FOUND A **PRESIDENTIAL CABINET** WITH A LOT OF DRAWERS IN IT...

THE **CONSTITUTION** SAYS OUR GOVERNMENT SHOULD ESTABLISH JUSTICE, ENSURE DOMESTIC PEACE, PROMOTE THE GENERAL WELFARE, AND PROVIDE DEFENSE. THE FOLKS IN THESE 15 DRAWERS DO ALL THAT ON A DAY-TO-DAY BASIS!

I HELP THE PRESIDENT DEAL WITH OTHER NATIONS. TOGETHER HE AND I DO THE FOREIGN POLICY OF OUR STATE.

Department of State
Est. 1789

TEXAS?

NO, NOT ONE OF THE 50 STATES — "STATE" CAN ALSO MEAN "**GOVERNMENT**" OR "NATION" OR "COLLECTIVE BODY" OR...

AS YOU CAN HEAR, SECRETARIES OF STATE USE UNUSUAL, FANCY WORDS. IT HELPS THEM TALK OUT OUR PROBLEMS WITH DIFFERENT CULTURES IN OTHER NATIONS. THIS IS A DELICATE JOB!

HERE'S AN OLD ARMY MAN!

"OLD?!" THE DEPARTMENT OF WAR WAS ONE OF THE **FIRST CREATED BY CONGRESS!** NOW I'M CALLED THE **SECRETARY OF DEFENSE** BECAUSE I RUN THE MILITARY THAT DEFENDS THE UNITED STATES AND ITS INTERESTS ACROSS THE WORLD.

Department of Defense
Est. 1789

I THOUGHT THE PRESIDENT WAS COMMANDER-IN-CHIEF OF THE ARMY.

HE IS. THE SECRETARY OF DEFENSE HELPS HIM MAKE DECISIONS — LIKE ALL THE MEMBERS OF THE CABINET DO FOR THE AREAS THEY COVER. THE D OF D IS THE **BIGGEST** CABINET POST, WITH ABOUT 3 MILLION EMPLOYEES!

oh, man...

AFTER THE TERRORIST ATTACKS OF 9-11, CONGRESS CREATED THIS DEPARTMENT TO DEAL WITH THREATS ON AMERICAN SOIL. I RUN THE COAST GUARD, BORDER PATROLS, AND AIRPORT SECURITY.

Department of Homeland Security
Est. 2003

AFTER THE SOLDIERS HAVE SERVED THEIR COUNTRY, I SERVE **THEM!** I GET THEM AND THEIR FAMILIES EDUCATION, HEALTH CARE, PENSIONS, AND PROPER MEMORIALS.

Department of Veterans Affairs
Est. 1989

next: **TREES & TURNIPS**

CHESTER THE CRAB
WHO GUARDS OUR TREES & CORN?

CHESTER THE CRAB

WHO WATCHES BIG (and small) BUSINESS?

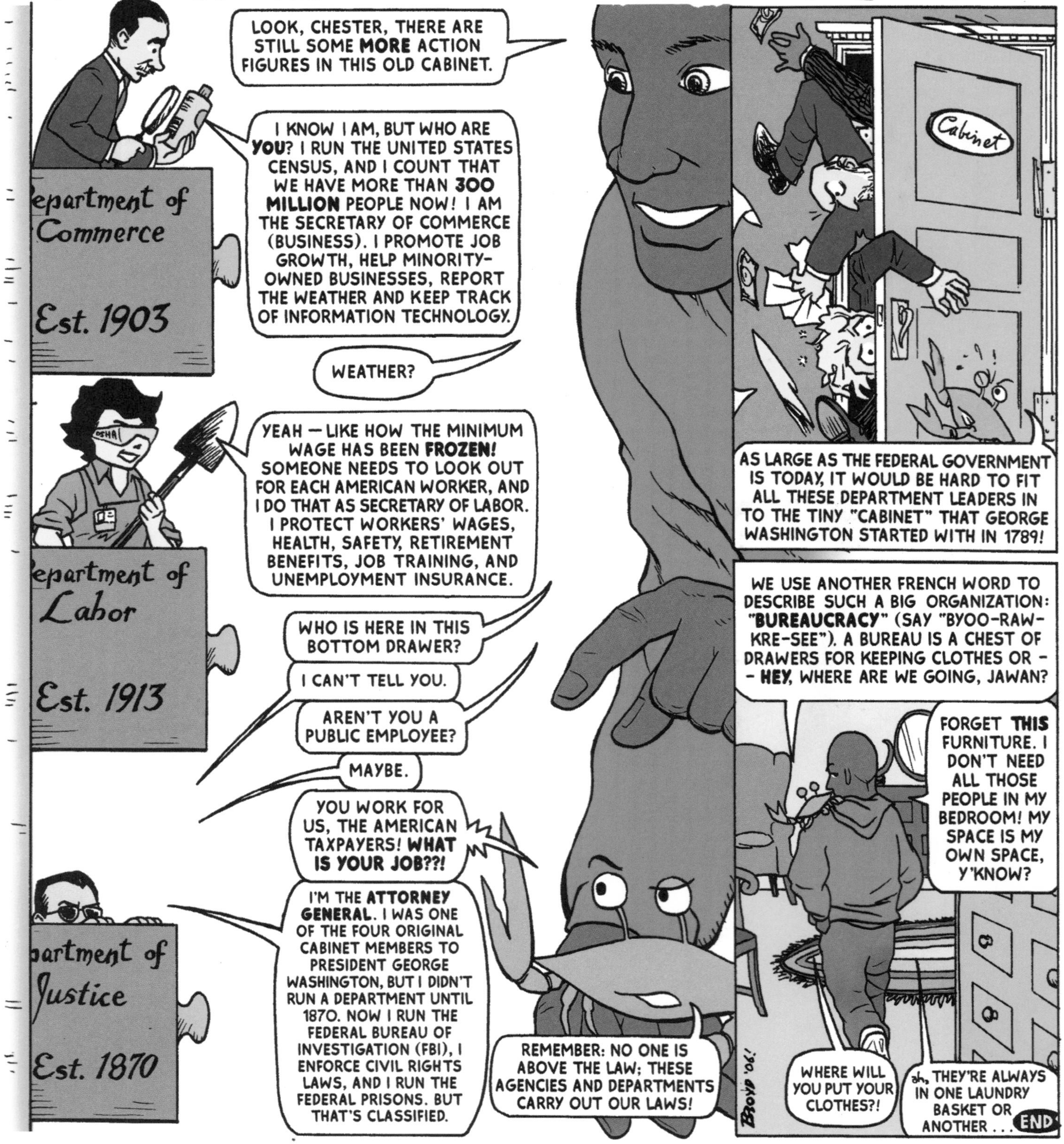